This book is to be

10 NOV 1

23

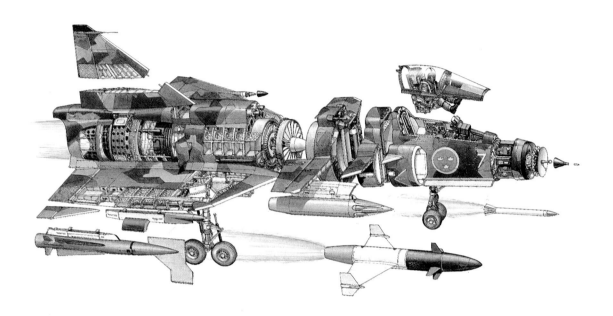

LOOK INSIDE
CROSS-SECTIONS
JETS

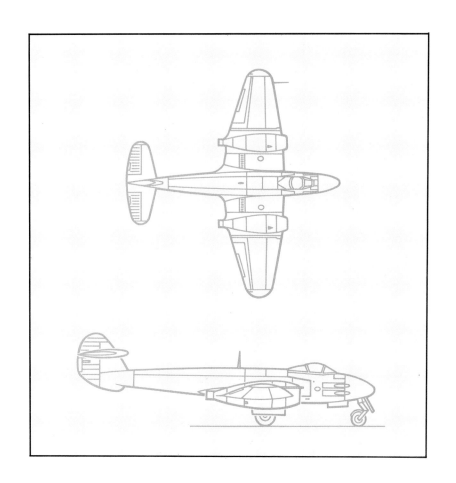

LOOK INSIDE
CROSS-SECTIONS
JETS

ILLUSTRATED BY
HANS JENSSEN
WRITTEN BY
MOIRA BUTTERFIELD

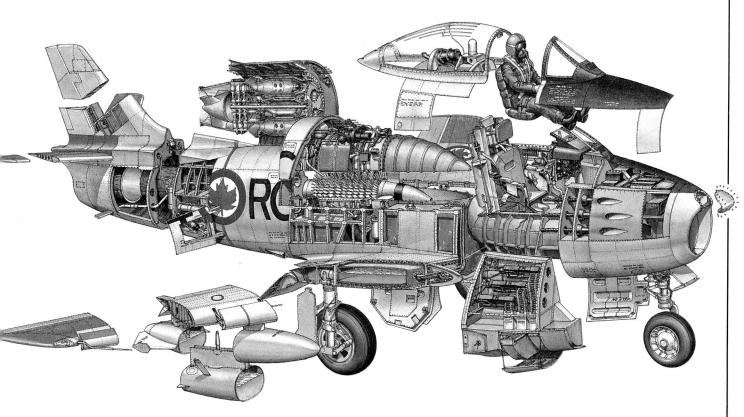

DORLING KINDERSLEY
LONDON • NEW YORK • STUTTGART

Senior Art Editor Dorian Spencer Davies
Designer Joanne Earl
Senior Editor John C. Miles
Editorial Assistant Nigel Ritchie
Deputy Art Director Miranda Kennedy
Deputy Editorial Director Sophie Mitchell
Production Charlotte Traill
Consultant Andrew Nahum
The Science Museum

First published in 1996
by Dorling Kindersley Limited,
9 Henrietta Street, London WC2E 8PS

A CIP catalogue record for this book is available
from the British Library

ISBN 0-7513-5439-2

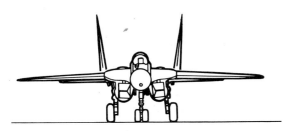

Reproduced by Dot Gradations, Essex
Printed and bound in Belgium by Proost

CONTENTS

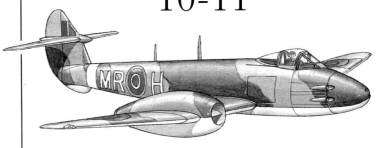

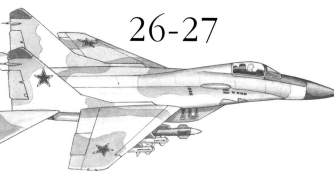

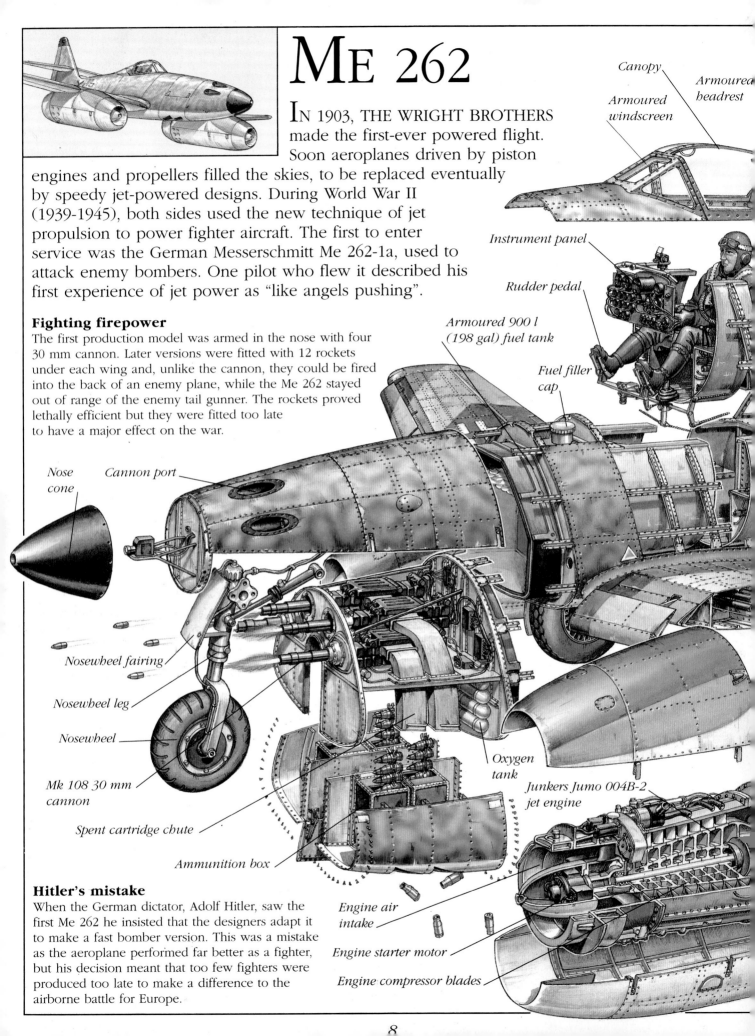

ME 262

IN 1903, THE WRIGHT BROTHERS made the first-ever powered flight. Soon aeroplanes driven by piston engines and propellers filled the skies, to be replaced eventually by speedy jet-powered designs. During World War II (1939-1945), both sides used the new technique of jet propulsion to power fighter aircraft. The first to enter service was the German Messerschmitt Me 262-1a, used to attack enemy bombers. One pilot who flew it described his first experience of jet power as "like angels pushing".

Fighting firepower

The first production model was armed in the nose with four 30 mm cannon. Later versions were fitted with 12 rockets under each wing and, unlike the cannon, they could be fired into the back of an enemy plane, while the Me 262 stayed out of range of the enemy tail gunner. The rockets proved lethally efficient but they were fitted too late to have a major effect on the war.

Canopy

Armoured headrest

Armoured windscreen

Instrument panel

Rudder pedal

Armoured 900 l (198 gal) fuel tank

Fuel filler cap

Nose cone

Cannon port

Nosewheel fairing

Nosewheel leg

Nosewheel

Mk 108 30 mm cannon

Spent cartridge chute

Ammunition box

Oxygen tank

Junkers Jumo 004B-2 jet engine

Engine air intake

Engine starter motor

Engine compressor blades

Hitler's mistake

When the German dictator, Adolf Hitler, saw the first Me 262 he insisted that the designers adapt it to make a fast bomber version. This was a mistake as the aeroplane performed far better as a fighter, but his decision meant that too few fighters were produced too late to make a difference to the airborne battle for Europe.

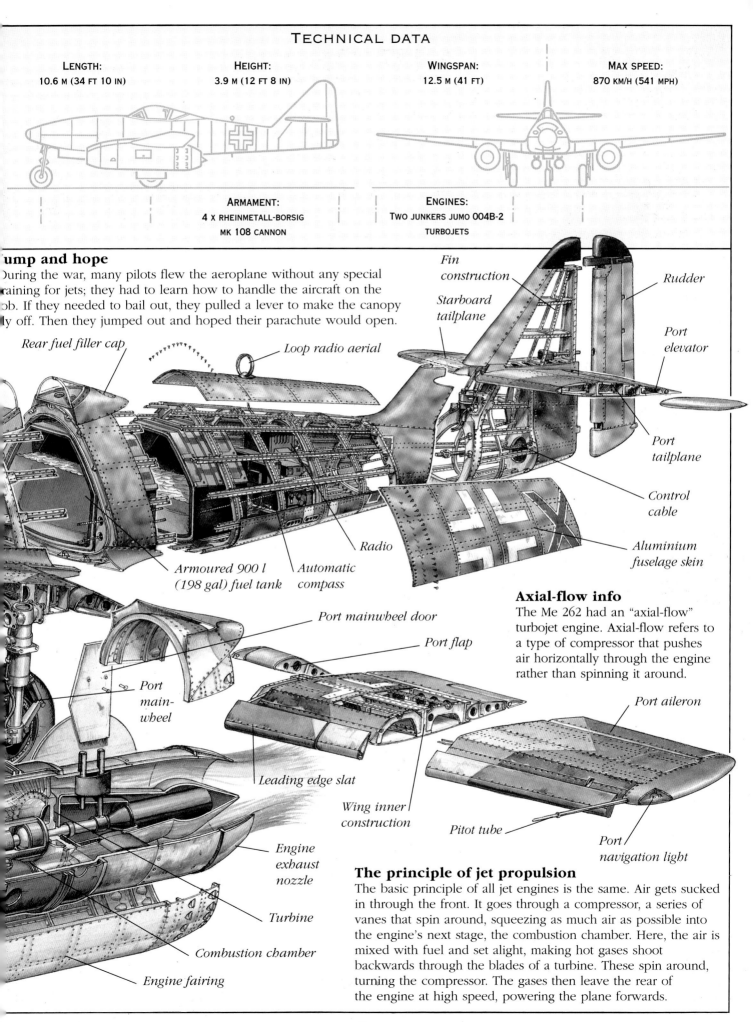

LENGTH:	HEIGHT:	WINGSPAN:	MAX SPEED:
10.6 M (34 FT 10 IN)	3.9 M (12 FT 8 IN)	12.5 M (41 FT)	870 KM/H (541 MPH)

ARMAMENT:	ENGINES:
4 X RHEINMETALL-BORSIG MK 108 CANNON	TWO JUNKERS JUMO 004B-2 TURBOJETS

ump and hope

During the war, many pilots flew the aeroplane without any special raining for jets; they had to learn how to handle the aircraft on the ob. If they needed to bail out, they pulled a lever to make the canopy ly off. Then they jumped out and hoped their parachute would open.

Rear fuel filler cap

Loop radio aerial

Fin construction

Starboard tailplane

Rudder

Port elevator

Port tailplane

Control cable

Radio

Aluminium fuselage skin

Armoured 900 l (198 gal) fuel tank

Automatic compass

Axial-flow info

The Me 262 had an "axial-flow" turbojet engine. Axial-flow refers to a type of compressor that pushes air horizontally through the engine rather than spinning it around.

Port mainwheel door

Port flap

Port aileron

Port mainwheel

Leading edge slat

Wing inner construction

Pitot tube

Port navigation light

Engine exhaust nozzle

Turbine

Combustion chamber

Engine fairing

The principle of jet propulsion

The basic principle of all jet engines is the same. Air gets sucked in through the front. It goes through a compressor, a series of vanes that spin around, squeezing as much air as possible into the engine's next stage, the combustion chamber. Here, the air is mixed with fuel and set alight, making hot gases shoot backwards through the blades of a turbine. These spin around, turning the compressor. The gases then leave the rear of the engine at high speed, powering the plane forwards.

GLOSTER METEOR

On a summer day in 1944, flight officer "Dixie" Dean of Britain's Royal Air Force made aviation history with his brand new plane, developed by the pioneering design team of Frank Whittle and George Carter. On a patrol flight Dean spotted a deadly robot V1 flying bomb speeding over the south coast of England towards London. He fired his cannon but they didn't work so he flew alongside, slid his plane's wingtip under the bomb and nudged it into a steep dive. Then he watched as it exploded harmlessly below. It was the first, but not the last, V1 to be destroyed by the Gloster Meteor, the first jet plane ever to work in an operational air force squadron.

Fuel flow
Early jets such as the Meteor were only refuelled on the ground. Fuel was pumped in from mobile tankers and it was a risky operation because if it was done wrongly an electrical charge could build up on the plane, causing an explosion. The ground crew had to wear rubber-soled boots to protect themselves from electric shocks and they used brass tools that wouldn't create sparks if they were dropped.

Identification markings
It is very important that pilots and ground gunners can easily recognize planes that are on their side. The best way to ensure this is to paint special markings on the planes. This wartime Meteor F1 had the roundels of the RAF and a group of small numbers and letters at the back to identify the particular plane.

All about wings
As a plane flies along, air flows over and under the wing. The upper wing surface is curved and the air flowing over it has a lower pressure than the air travelling under the flat surface below the wing. The air beneath pushes upwards with a force called "upthrust", giving the plane enough lift to stay airborne.

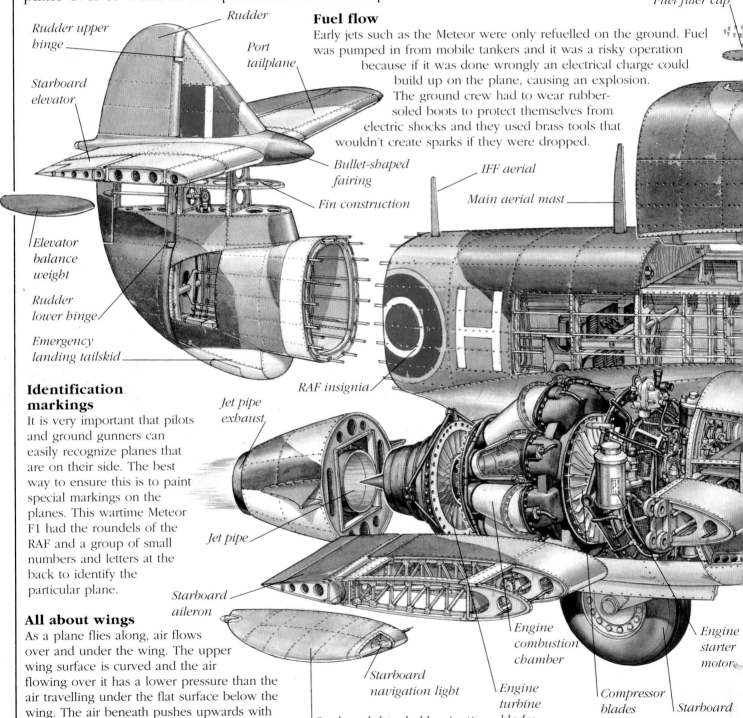

Rudder upper hinge

Rudder

Port tailplane

Starboard elevator

Elevator balance weight

Rudder lower hinge

Emergency landing tailskid

Bullet-shaped fairing

Fin construction

Fuel filler cap

IFF aerial

Main aerial mast

RAF insignia

Jet pipe exhaust

Jet pipe

Starboard aileron

Starboard navigation light

Starboard detachable wingtip

Engine combustion chamber

Engine turbine blades

Compressor blades

Engine starter motor

Starboard mainwheel

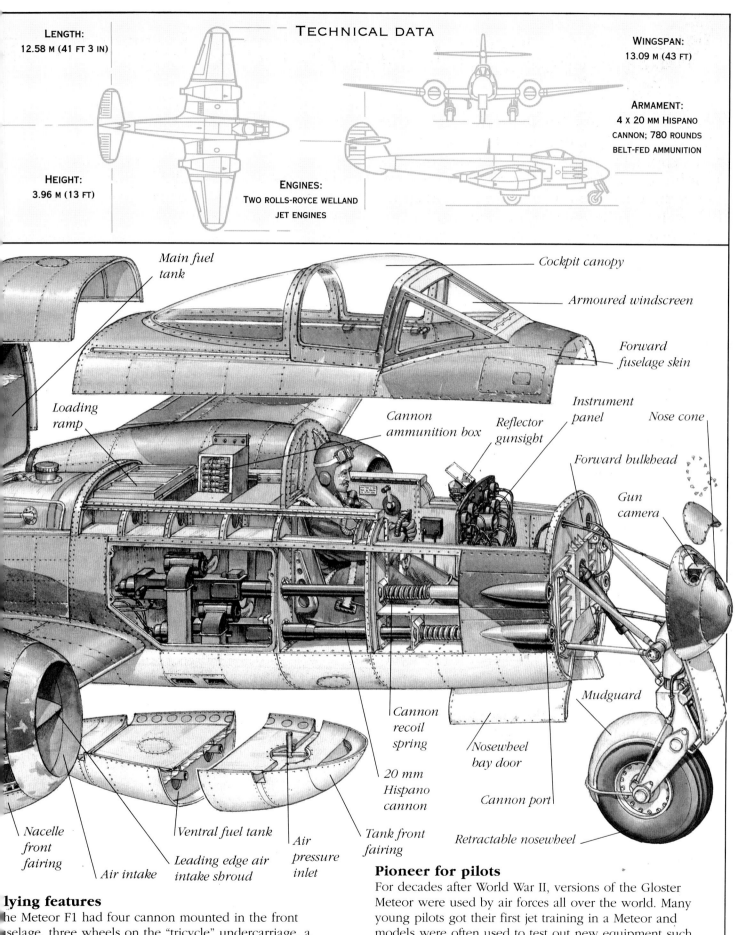

LENGTH:
12.58 M (41 FT 3 IN)

HEIGHT:
3.96 M (13 FT)

ENGINES:
TWO ROLLS-ROYCE WELLAND
JET ENGINES

WINGSPAN:
13.09 M (43 FT)

ARMAMENT:
4 x 20 MM HISPANO
CANNON; 780 ROUNDS
BELT-FED AMMUNITION

Main fuel tank

Cockpit canopy

Armoured windscreen

Forward fuselage skin

Loading ramp

Cannon ammunition box

Reflector gunsight

Instrument panel

Nose cone

Forward bulkhead

Gun camera

Cannon recoil spring

20 mm Hispano cannon

Tank front fairing

Nosewheel bay door

Cannon port

Mudguard

Retractable nosewheel

Nacelle front fairing

Air intake

Ventral fuel tank

Leading edge air intake shroud

Air pressure inlet

Flying features

The Meteor F1 had four cannon mounted in the front fuselage, three wheels on the "tricycle" undercarriage, a tailplane set high up at the back, and two engines mounted on the wings. Each engine was fitted inside a streamlined metal casing called a nacelle.

Pioneer for pilots

For decades after World War II, versions of the Gloster Meteor were used by air forces all over the world. Many young pilots got their first jet training in a Meteor and models were often used to test out new equipment such as ejection seats. In the years just after the war, a succession of Meteors held the world airspeed record, flying at over 990 km/h (600 mph).

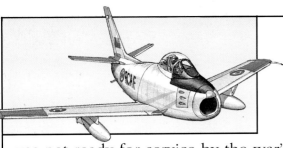

F-86 SABRE

THE DESIGN THAT BECAME THE US F-86 SABRE originated during World War II. However, this fighter was not ready for service by the war's end. The North American Aviation company waited so that their designers could use research captured from the Germans. The prototype (first) Sabre flew on 1 October 1947, and three years later developed versions saw combat in the Korean War (1950-53). After the Korean War, versions of the F-86 were bought by many countries and remained in service throughout the 1960s. The picture below shows a Canadair Sabre 6 of the Royal Canadian Air Force.

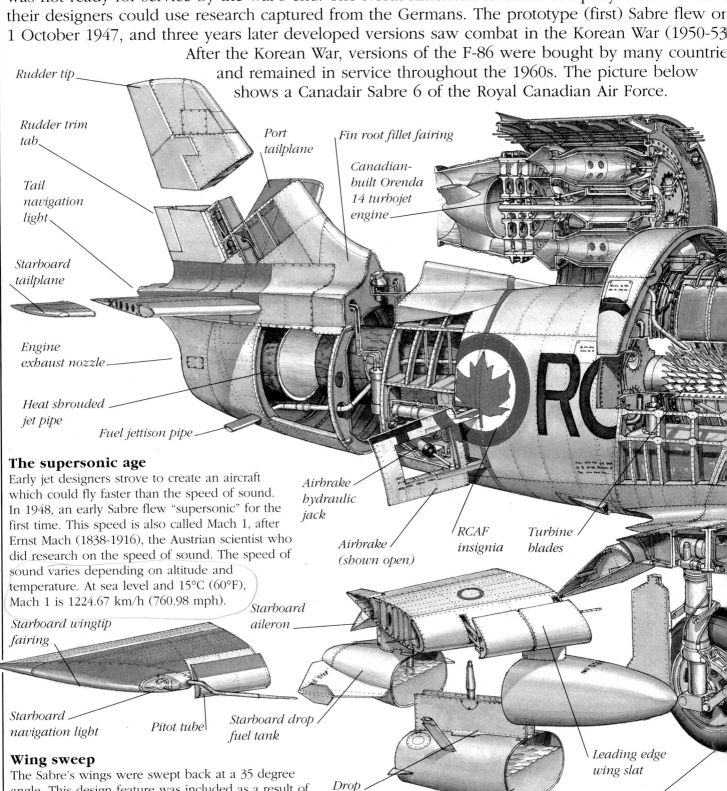

Rudder tip

Rudder trim tab

Tail navigation light

Starboard tailplane

Engine exhaust nozzle

Heat shrouded jet pipe

Fuel jettison pipe

Port tailplane

Fin root fillet fairing

Canadian-built Orenda 14 turbojet engine

Airbrake hydraulic jack

Airbrake (shown open)

RCAF insignia

Turbine blades

The supersonic age

Early jet designers strove to create an aircraft which could fly faster than the speed of sound. In 1948, an early Sabre flew "supersonic" for the first time. This speed is also called Mach 1, after Ernst Mach (1838-1916), the Austrian scientist who did research on the speed of sound. The speed of sound varies depending on altitude and temperature. At sea level and 15°C (60°F), Mach 1 is 1224.67 km/h (760.98 mph).

Starboard wingtip fairing

Starboard navigation light

Pitot tube

Starboard aileron

Starboard drop fuel tank

Drop tank pylon

Jet fuel

Leading edge wing slat

Starboard mainwheel

Wing sweep

The Sabre's wings were swept back at a 35 degree angle. This design feature was included as a result of German research, which indicated that jet aircraft performed better and could reach higher speeds if the wings were angled back from the fuselage.

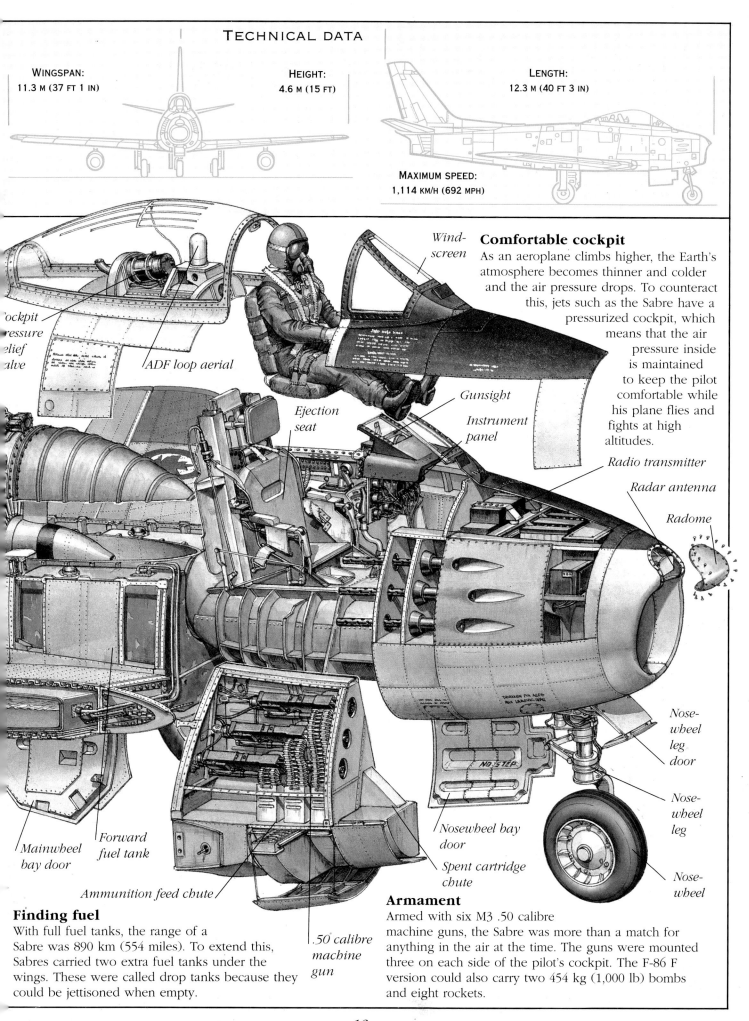

TECHNICAL DATA

WINGSPAN:
11.3 M (37 FT 1 IN)

HEIGHT:
4.6 M (15 FT)

LENGTH:
12.3 M (40 FT 3 IN)

MAXIMUM SPEED:
1,114 KM/H (692 MPH)

Cockpit
pressure
relief
valve

ADF loop aerial

Ejection
seat

Wind-
screen

Gunsight

Instrument
panel

Radio transmitter

Radar antenna

Radome

Nose-
wheel
leg
door

Nose-
wheel
leg

Nose-
wheel

Nosewheel bay
door

Spent cartridge
chute

Mainwheel
bay door

Forward
fuel tank

Ammunition feed chute

.50 calibre
machine
gun

Comfortable cockpit

As an aeroplane climbs higher, the Earth's atmosphere becomes thinner and colder and the air pressure drops. To counteract this, jets such as the Sabre have a pressurized cockpit, which means that the air pressure inside is maintained to keep the pilot comfortable while his plane flies and fights at high altitudes.

Finding fuel

With full fuel tanks, the range of a Sabre was 890 km (554 miles). To extend this, Sabres carried two extra fuel tanks under the wings. These were called drop tanks because they could be jettisoned when empty.

Armament

Armed with six M3 .50 calibre machine guns, the Sabre was more than a match for anything in the air at the time. The guns were mounted three on each side of the pilot's cockpit. The F-86 F version could also carry two 454 kg (1,000 lb) bombs and eight rockets.

A-10 THUNDERBOLT

ONE OF THE MOST UNUSUAL JET AIRCRAFT IN SERVICE today, the odd look of the A-10 Thunderbolt led to its being nicknamed "Warthog", a kind of wild pig renowned for being ugly and fierce! Developed in the 1970s, the plane is still in use by US forces around the world. Like its animal namesake, the A-10 forages near the ground, its mission to destroy enemy tanks. It is equipped with a formidable array of weapons, and cruises above the battlefield. Once an enemy tank is located, the pilot destroys it with the rapid-fire 30 mm cannon or air-to-ground missiles.

Extra armour

Inside the cockpit, the pilot is surrounded by super-strong titanium-alloy armour up to 38 mm (1.5 in) thick. This protects the pilot against hits from the ground when the "Warthog" is flying in low to attack a tank.

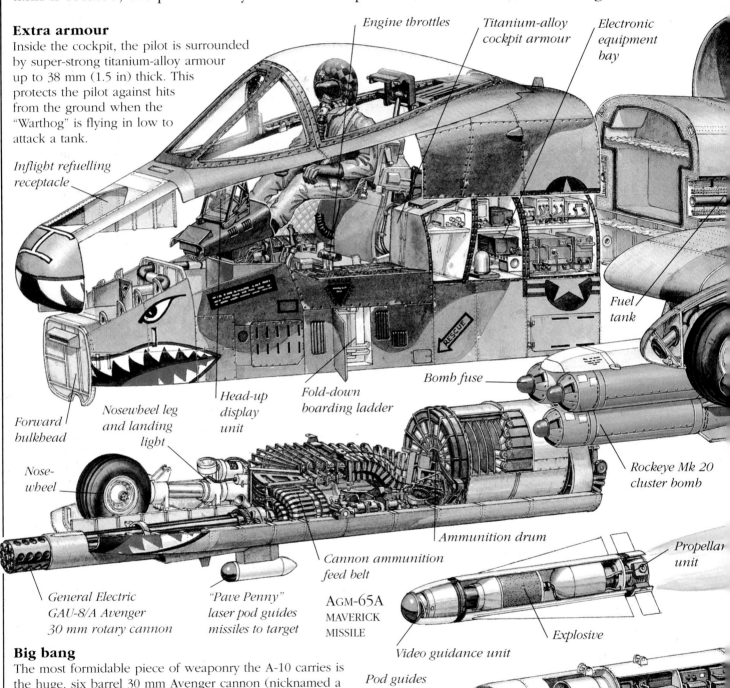

Engine throttles

Titanium-alloy cockpit armour

Electronic equipment bay

Inflight refuelling receptacle

Fuel tank

Bomb fuse

Rockeye Mk 20 cluster bomb

Forward bulkhead

Nosewheel leg and landing light

Head-up display unit

Fold-down boarding ladder

Nose-wheel

Ammunition drum

Cannon ammunition feed belt

Propellant unit

General Electric GAU-8/A Avenger 30 mm rotary cannon

"Pave Penny" laser pod guides missiles to target

AGM-65A MAVERICK MISSILE

Explosive

Video guidance unit

Big bang

The most formidable piece of weaponry the A-10 carries is the huge, six barrel 30 mm Avenger cannon (nicknamed a "burp gun" because of the noise it makes). It can fire up to 4,200 rounds a minute, and is loaded with high explosive or armour-piercing shells. The armour-piercing shells have a uranium core which is very dense. This means that the shells are able to blast through armour plate on enemy tanks.

Pod guides Maverick missiles and Paveway bombs to targets on ground

LANTIRN TARGETING POD

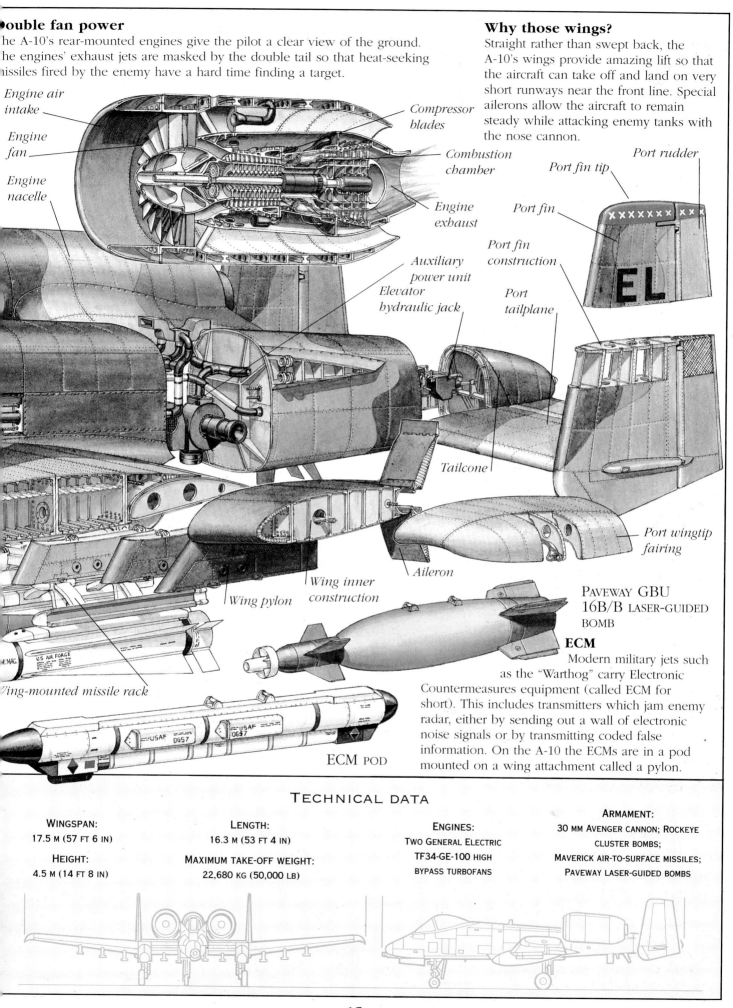

Double fan power

The A-10's rear-mounted engines give the pilot a clear view of the ground. The engines' exhaust jets are masked by the double tail so that heat-seeking missiles fired by the enemy have a hard time finding a target.

Engine air intake

Engine fan

Engine nacelle

Compressor blades

Combustion chamber

Engine exhaust

Auxiliary power unit

Elevator hydraulic jack

Tailcone

Wing pylon

Wing inner construction

Aileron

Wing-mounted missile rack

Why those wings?

Straight rather than swept back, the A-10's wings provide amazing lift so that the aircraft can take off and land on very short runways near the front line. Special ailerons allow the aircraft to remain steady while attacking enemy tanks with the nose cannon.

Port rudder

Port fin tip

Port fin

Port fin construction

Port tailplane

Port wingtip fairing

PAVEWAY GBU 16B/B LASER-GUIDED BOMB

ECM

Modern military jets such as the "Warthog" carry Electronic Countermeasures equipment (called ECM for short). This includes transmitters which jam enemy radar, either by sending out a wall of electronic noise signals or by transmitting coded false information. On the A-10 the ECMs are in a pod mounted on a wing attachment called a pylon.

ECM POD

TECHNICAL DATA

WINGSPAN:
17.5 M (57 FT 6 IN)

HEIGHT:
4.5 M (14 FT 8 IN)

LENGTH:
16.3 M (53 FT 4 IN)

MAXIMUM TAKE-OFF WEIGHT:
22,680 KG (50,000 LB)

ENGINES:
TWO GENERAL ELECTRIC
TF34-GE-100 HIGH
BYPASS TURBOFANS

ARMAMENT:
30 MM AVENGER CANNON; ROCKEYE
CLUSTER BOMBS;
MAVERICK AIR-TO-SURFACE MISSILES;
PAVEWAY LASER-GUIDED BOMBS

STARFIGHTER

LOOKING ALMOST LIKE A PILOTED MISSILE, THE Lockheed F-104 Starfighter originated during the Korean War (1950-53). The chief designer at Lockheed, C.L. "Kelly" Johnson, talked to pilots returning from the war and began to design a jet fighter for the US Air Force which would be faster than anything being flown by enemy forces. The aircraft which emerged four years later had wings only 10 cm (4 in) thick to reduce drag (air resistance) at high supersonic speeds. Early versions of the Starfighter were dogged by accidents and a high crash rate, but later versions were more successful and were bought by countries such as Germany, Italy, Canada, and Japan for their air forces.

HUD

Some Starfighter versions were among the first planes to be fitted with head-up display (HUD for short) in the cockpit. In a jet fighter with HUD, vital information from the control dials and displays is projected on to the windscreen, so the pilot does not have to look down while flying.

Unusual ejection

The first F-104s were fitted with a downward-firing ejector seat, because the more usual upward-firing version might have hit the extra-high tailplane. If a pilot needs to eject, he must grab for a handle. In a split second the seat's gun cartridge fires to propel it out of the plane.

All about missiles

Missiles fired by aircraft fall into two categories. Jets fire air-to-air missiles at other jets to destroy them. The Starfighter carried up to four Sidewinder air-to-air missiles. These were heat-seeking; the missile homed in on the enemy aircraft's hot exhaust jet. Aircraft also fire air-to-ground missiles. These destroy enemy targets on the ground below and are now usually directed by lasers to their target.

SIDEWINDER AIR-TO-AIR MISSILE

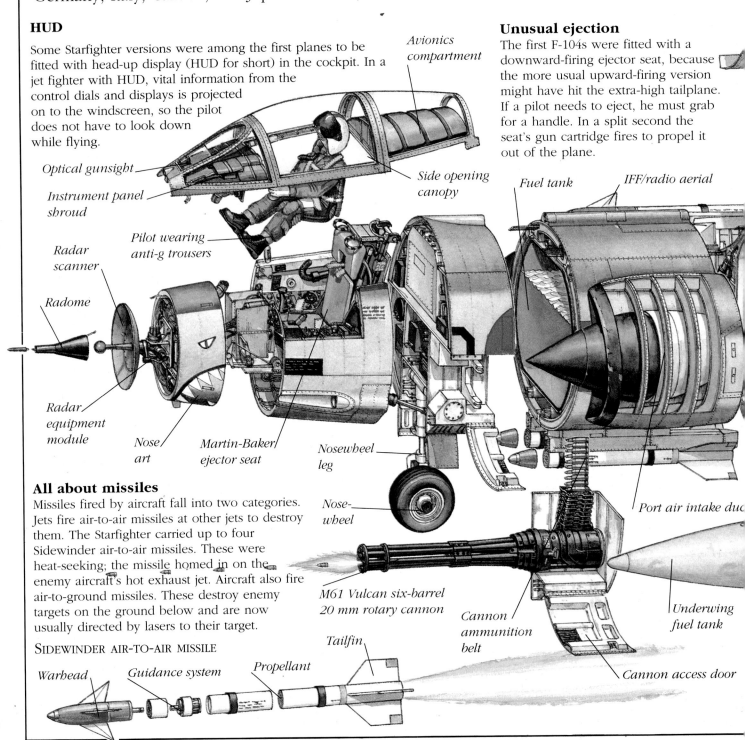

Avionics compartment

Side opening canopy

Optical gunsight

Instrument panel shroud

Radar scanner

Pilot wearing anti-g trousers

Radome

Fuel tank

IFF/radio aerial

Radar equipment module

Nose art

Martin-Baker ejector seat

Nosewheel leg

Nose-wheel

Port air intake duct

M61 Vulcan six-barrel 20 mm rotary cannon

Cannon ammunition belt

Underwing fuel tank

Tailfin

Cannon access door

Warhead

Guidance system

Propellant

Technical data

Wingspan:
6.7 M (21 FT 11 IN)

Height:
4.2 M (13 FT 6 IN)

Length:
16.7 M (54 FT 9 IN)

Maximum speed:
2,092 KM/H (1,300 MPH)

Engine:
ONE GENERAL ELECTRIC J79-GE-19
AFTERBURNING TURBOJET

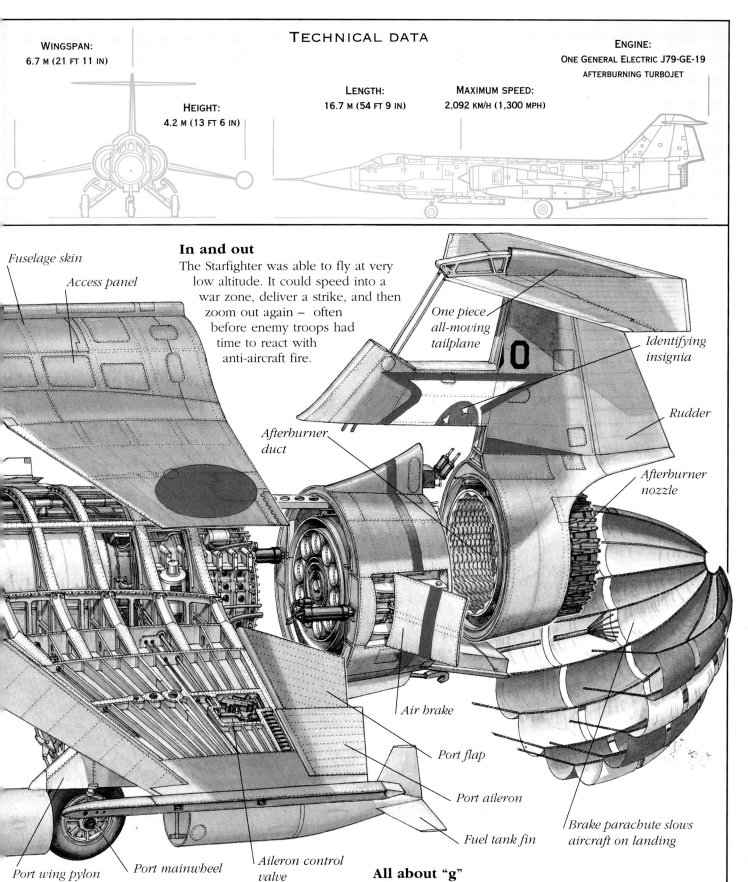

In and out

The Starfighter was able to fly at very low altitude. It could speed into a war zone, deliver a strike, and then zoom out again – often before enemy troops had time to react with anti-aircraft fire.

Fuselage skin

Access panel

One piece all-moving tailplane

Identifying insignia

Rudder

Afterburner duct

Afterburner nozzle

Air brake

Port flap

Port aileron

Fuel tank fin

Brake parachute slows aircraft on landing

Port wing pylon

Port mainwheel

Aileron control valve

peedy engine

arly jet engines lacked the power to push aircraft to double e speed of sound. When C.L. Johnson began to design the -104 in the early 1950s, there was no jet engine powerful nough to reach the speeds he envisioned. Fortunately, eneral Electric was developing the powerful J79 turbojet at e same time, and this became the engine of the F-104.

All about "g"

When a military jet plane accelerates upwards or turns, the force of gravity pulls down harder on the plane and the pilot. This causes a force on the body called "g". Without the right clothing, the pilot would black out as "g" stops the blood circulating properly. To prevent this, a jet pilot wears "anti-g" trousers, which contain inflatable pads. The trousers are attached to an air supply, so that the pads inflate to force blood back up to the heart.

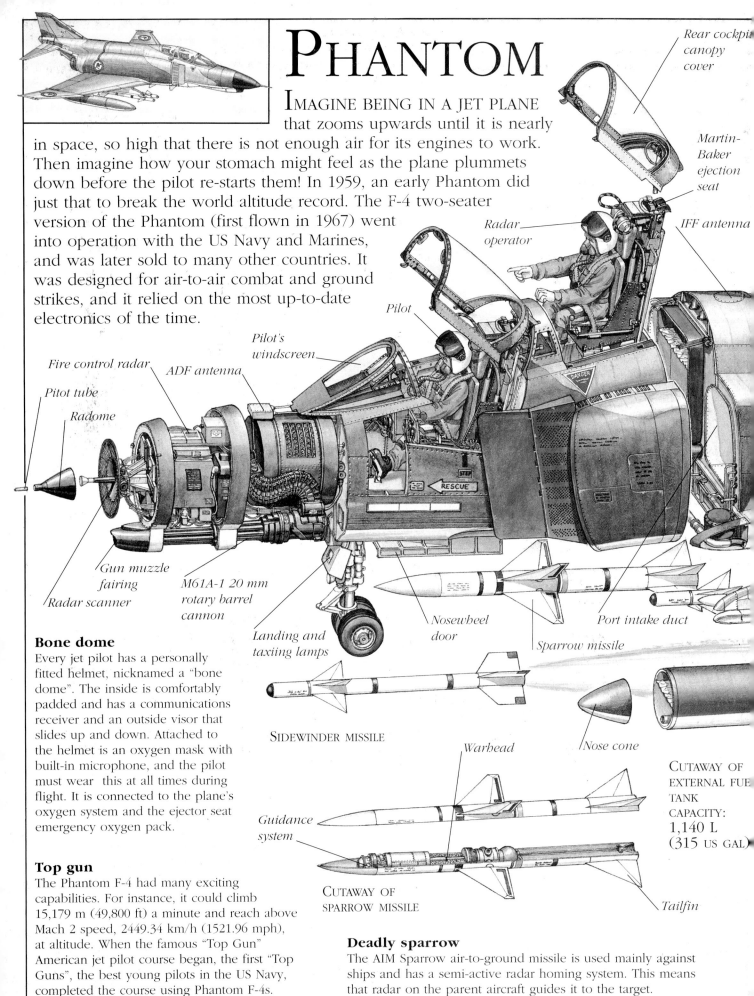

PHANTOM

IMAGINE BEING IN A JET PLANE that zooms upwards until it is nearly in space, so high that there is not enough air for its engines to work. Then imagine how your stomach might feel as the plane plummets down before the pilot re-starts them! In 1959, an early Phantom did just that to break the world altitude record. The F-4 two-seater version of the Phantom (first flown in 1967) went into operation with the US Navy and Marines, and was later sold to many other countries. It was designed for air-to-air combat and ground strikes, and it relied on the most up-to-date electronics of the time.

Rear cockpit canopy cover

Martin-Baker ejection seat

IFF antenna

Radar operator

Pilot

Pilot's windscreen

Fire control radar

ADF antenna

Pitot tube

Radome

DANGER

STEP

RESCUE

Gun muzzle fairing

M61A-1 20 mm rotary barrel cannon

Radar scanner

Landing and taxiing lamps

Nosewheel door

Port intake duct

Sparrow missile

SIDEWINDER MISSILE

Warhead

Nose cone

CUTAWAY OF EXTERNAL FUEL TANK CAPACITY: 1,140 L (315 US GAL)

Guidance system

CUTAWAY OF SPARROW MISSILE

Tailfin

Bone dome

Every jet pilot has a personally fitted helmet, nicknamed a "bone dome". The inside is comfortably padded and has a communications receiver and an outside visor that slides up and down. Attached to the helmet is an oxygen mask with built-in microphone, and the pilot must wear this at all times during flight. It is connected to the plane's oxygen system and the ejector seat emergency oxygen pack.

Top gun

The Phantom F-4 had many exciting capabilities. For instance, it could climb 15,179 m (49,800 ft) a minute and reach above Mach 2 speed, 2449.34 km/h (1521.96 mph), at altitude. When the famous "Top Gun" American jet pilot course began, the first "Top Guns", the best young pilots in the US Navy, completed the course using Phantom F-4s.

Deadly sparrow

The AIM Sparrow air-to-ground missile is used mainly against ships and has a semi-active radar homing system. This means that radar on the parent aircraft guides it to the target.

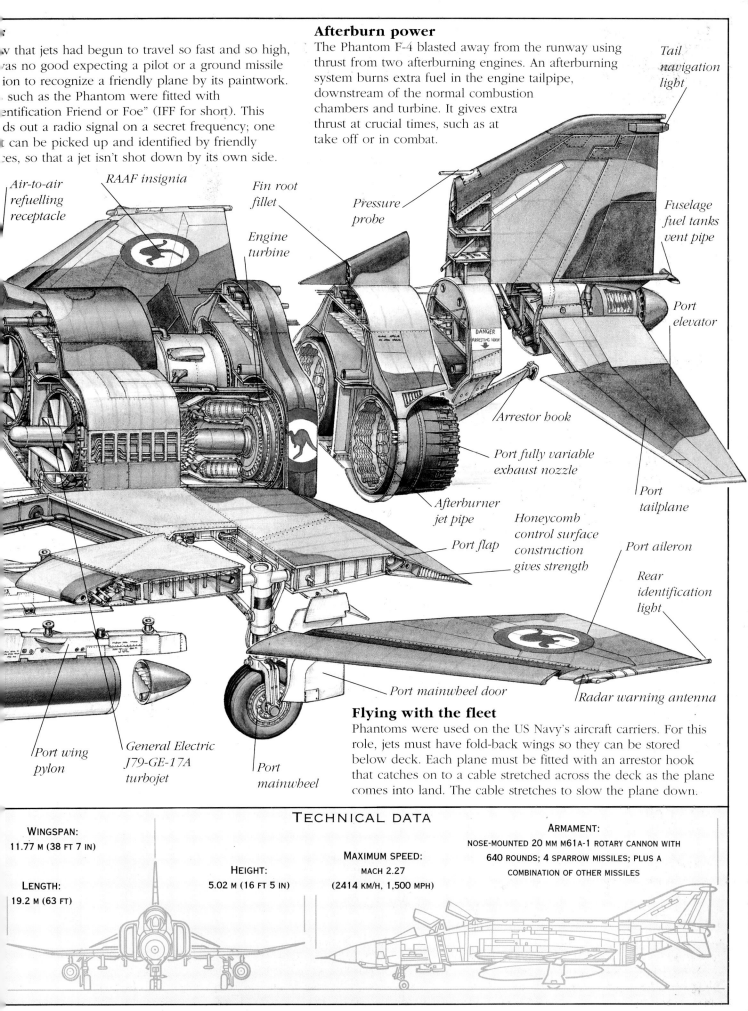

Afterburn power

The Phantom F-4 blasted away from the runway using thrust from two afterburning engines. An afterburning system burns extra fuel in the engine tailpipe, downstream of the normal combustion chambers and turbine. It gives extra thrust at crucial times, such as at take off or in combat.

that jets had begun to travel so fast and so high,
as no good expecting a pilot or a ground missile
ion to recognize a friendly plane by its paintwork.
such as the Phantom were fitted with
entification Friend or Foe" (IFF for short). This
ds out a radio signal on a secret frequency; one
can be picked up and identified by friendly
es, so that a jet isn't shot down by its own side.

Air-to-air refuelling receptacle

RAAF insignia

Fin root fillet

Engine turbine

Pressure probe

Tail navigation light

Fuselage fuel tanks vent pipe

Port elevator

Arrestor hook

Port fully variable exhaust nozzle

Afterburner jet pipe

Port flap

Honeycomb control surface construction gives strength

Port tailplane

Port aileron

Rear identification light

Port mainwheel door

Radar warning antenna

Port wing pylon

General Electric J79-GE-17A turbojet

Port mainwheel

Flying with the fleet

Phantoms were used on the US Navy's aircraft carriers. For this role, jets must have fold-back wings so they can be stored below deck. Each plane must be fitted with an arrestor hook that catches on to a cable stretched across the deck as the plane comes into land. The cable stretches to slow the plane down.

TECHNICAL DATA

WINGSPAN:
11.77 M (38 FT 7 IN)

LENGTH:
19.2 M (63 FT)

HEIGHT:
5.02 M (16 FT 5 IN)

MAXIMUM SPEED:
MACH 2.27
(2414 KM/H, 1,500 MPH)

ARMAMENT:
NOSE-MOUNTED 20 MM M61A-1 ROTARY CANNON WITH 640 ROUNDS; 4 SPARROW MISSILES; PLUS A COMBINATION OF OTHER MISSILES

MIRAGE

IN 1984, THE FRENCH AIR FORCE, THE *ARMÉE DE L'AIR*, took delivery of its first Mirage 2000C. Intended to be used mainly to intercept enemy planes or missiles, its design shows the difference between the first fighter jets and the modern versions. By the time the Mirage flew, manoeuvrability was much more important than attaining ever higher speeds. The agile Mirage 2000 can fly at more than Mach 2 at high altitude, but it can also perform well at low speed and has a very good rate of climb, enabling it to attack a high altitude target quickly. Armed with powerful radar and computer technology, modern jets such as the Mirage take many years to develop. Each plane costs millions to build.

Radio and electronics

IFF/radio aerial

SAUVETAGE

Instrument panel shroud

Frameless windscreen panel

Fixed in-flight refuelling probe

Glass-fibre radome

Pilot's head-up display unit (HUD)

Pitot tube

Flat-plate radar scanner

Multi-role radar unit

Angle of attack probe

Pulse doppler radar unit

2-EF

Ejection seat

Forward port integral fuel tank

Port side console panel

Landing and taxiing lamps

Towing bracket

30 mm DEFA cannon

Fly-by-wire

In an early jet fighter, the pilot would pull on a control column and push on rudder pedals to operate hydraulic systems which moved the control surfaces directly in response. In a "fly-by-wire" system, the pilot's controls send signals to an on-board computer and this alters the plane's course.

TECHNICAL DATA

MAXIMUM SPEED:
MACH 2.3 (2,445 KM/H, 1,520 MPH)

WINGSPAN:
9.02 M (29 FT 6 IN)

HEIGHT:
3.4 M (11 FT 2 IN)

ENGINE:
SNECMA M53-5 AFTERBURNING TURBOFAN

LENGTH:
15.33 M (50 FT 3 IN)

ARMAMENT:
2 X 30 MM DEFA CANNON; COMBINATION OF MISSILES

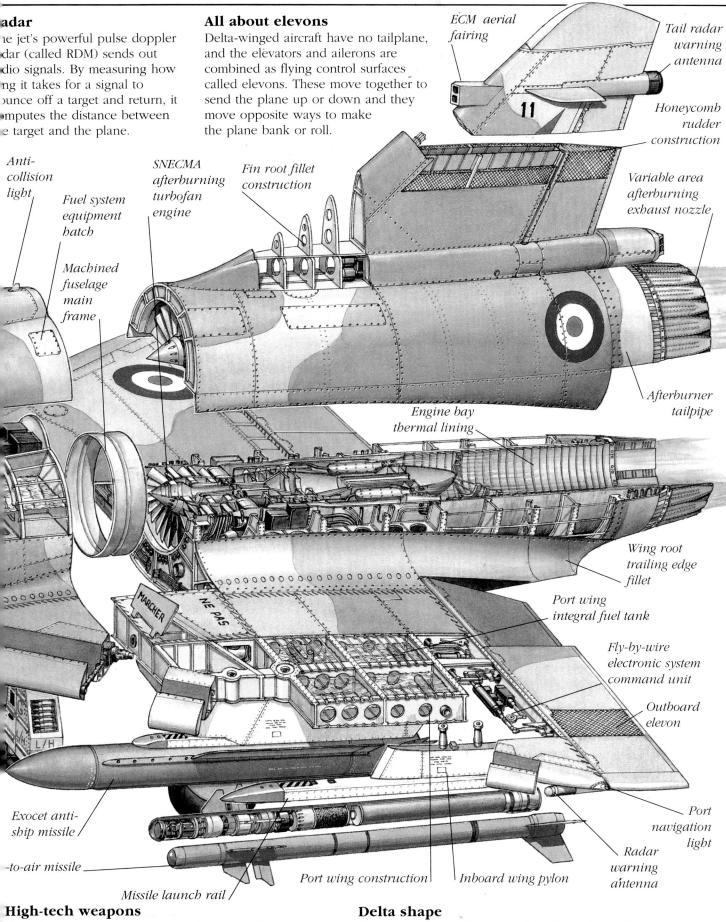

adar

e jet's powerful pulse doppler
dar (called RDM) sends out
dio signals. By measuring how
ng it takes for a signal to
ounce off a target and return, it
mputes the distance between
e target and the plane.

All about elevons

Delta-winged aircraft have no tailplane,
and the elevators and ailerons are
combined as flying control surfaces
called elevons. These move together to
send the plane up or down and they
move opposite ways to make
the plane bank or roll.

ECM aerial fairing

Tail radar warning antenna

Honeycomb rudder construction

Anti-collision light

Fuel system equipment hatch

SNECMA afterburning turbofan engine

Fin root fillet construction

Machined fuselage main frame

Variable area afterburning exhaust nozzle

Engine bay thermal lining

Afterburner tailpipe

Wing root trailing edge fillet

Port wing integral fuel tank

Fly-by-wire electronic system command unit

Outboard elevon

Exocet anti-ship missile

-to-air missile

Missile launch rail

Port wing construction

Inboard wing pylon

Radar warning antenna

Port navigation light

High-tech weapons

The Mirage can carry various combinations of weapons
under its wings and fuselage, including radar-guided or
infra-red heat-seeking missiles and laser-guided bombs,
which travel along a laser beam directed at a target.

Delta shape

The wings of the Mirage are delta-shaped, which means they
are triangular. They help to reduce drag (air resistance) at high
speed and so increase the aeroplane's agility. They are smaller
than ordinary wings and more difficult to detect on radar.

F-14A TOMCAT

A GIANT US NAVY AIRCRAFT CARRIER IS ON A MILITARY exercise when its fighter jets are ordered into the air to practise defending the fleet from enemy attack. The deck crews spring into action and in a few minutes a squadron of F-14 fighters is airborne. Such a scene could have taken place at any time since the 1970s when the first F-14 versions appeared. Fast and powerfully armed, they became the main long-range defence aircraft of the US fleet.

Talking tactics

Like other jet fighters, F-14s fly in groups of at least two. They may need to talk to their fellow aircrews, but they don't want to give their position away to the enemy so they talk on a secure radio link that is very hard to locate or jam.

Super system

F-14As were followed by F-14D Super Tomcats with more powerful engines, and radar that could track 24 targets.

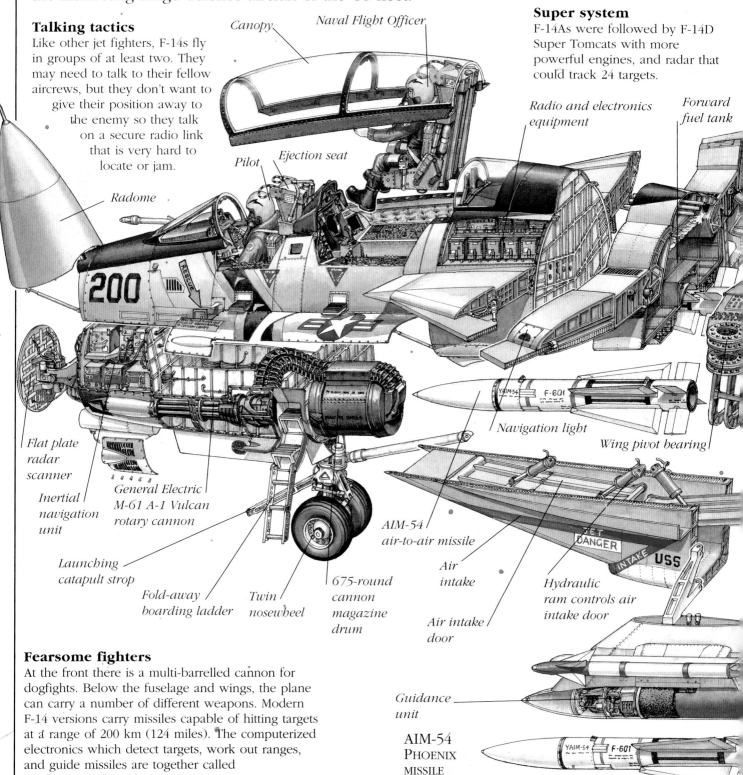

Canopy

Naval Flight Officer

Radio and electronics equipment

Forward fuel tank

Pilot

Ejection seat

Radome

200

Navigation light

Wing pivot bearing

Flat plate radar scanner

Inertial navigation unit

General Electric M-61 A-1 Vulcan rotary cannon

Launching catapult strop

Fold-away boarding ladder

Twin nosewheel

675-round cannon magazine drum

AIM-54 air-to-air missile

Air intake

Air intake door

Hydraulic ram controls air intake door

Guidance unit

AIM-54 PHOENIX MISSILE

Fearsome fighters

At the front there is a multi-barrelled cannon for dogfights. Below the fuselage and wings, the plane can carry a number of different weapons. Modern F-14 versions carry missiles capable of hitting targets at a range of 200 km (124 miles). The computerized electronics which detect targets, work out ranges, and guide missiles are together called the fire-control system.

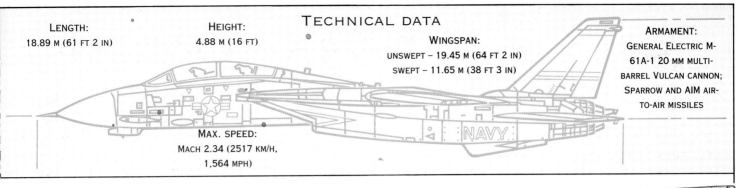

LENGTH:
18.89 M (61 FT 2 IN)

HEIGHT:
4.88 M (16 FT)

WINGSPAN:
UNSWEPT – 19.45 M (64 FT 2 IN)
SWEPT – 11.65 M (38 FT 3 IN)

ARMAMENT:
GENERAL ELECTRIC M-61A-1 20 MM MULTI-BARREL VULCAN CANNON; SPARROW AND AIM AIR-TO-AIR MISSILES

MAX. SPEED:
MACH 2.34 (2517 KM/H, 1,564 MPH)

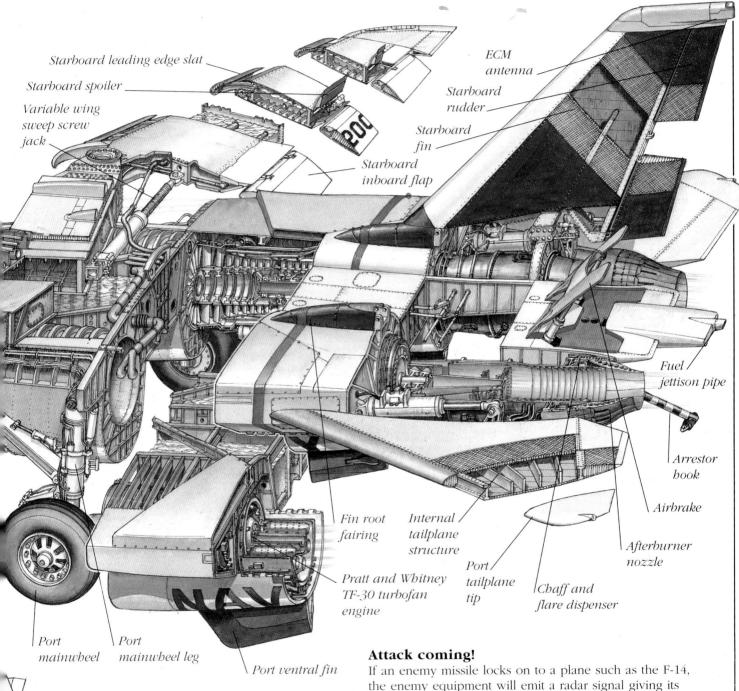

Starboard leading edge slat

Starboard spoiler

Variable wing sweep screw jack

ECM antenna

Starboard rudder

Starboard fin

Starboard inboard flap

Fuel jettison pipe

Arrestor hook

Airbrake

Afterburner nozzle

Fin root fairing

Internal tailplane structure

Port tailplane tip

Chaff and flare dispenser

Pratt and Whitney TF-30 turbofan engine

Port mainwheel

Port mainwheel leg

Port ventral fin

Swing wing

The Tomcat is a "variable geometry" or "swing wing" aircraft, which means it can change its shape by sweeping its wings backwards. The onboard computerized flight control system alters the plane's outline in this way to change its performance in the air.

Attack coming!

If an enemy missile locks on to a plane such as the F-14, the enemy equipment will emit a radar signal giving its position away. The F-14 may be armed with anti-radiation missiles that can home in on the enemy signal. If not, the pilot could try to fly out of the missile's range, or operate his chaff and flare dispenser. This sends out flares to confuse heat-seeking missiles or a plume of metal particles (chaff) that hangs in the air and fool a radar-seeking missile, directing it away from the plane.

SAAB VIGGEN

IF AN ENEMY WERE EVER TO THREATEN SWEDEN, one of the world's most formidable fighter jets, the Saab Viggen JA37, would emerge from underground hangars dotted over the country. The Viggen, the Swedish word for "thunderbolt", is a multi-role jet, which means it can do several different jobs. Most importantly, it doesn't need to operate from a big airfield. It is designed for STOL (Short Take Off and Landing) on runways or stretches of road hidden in the dense Scandinavian forests

Stopping fast
As soon as the plane's nosewheel touches the ground on landing, a thrust-reverser cuts into the turbofan engine. This deflects the exhaust forwards through nozzles in the fuselage, helping to brake the plane quickly. It's possible to land an JA37 on a slippery icebound runway only 500 m (1,640 ft) long.

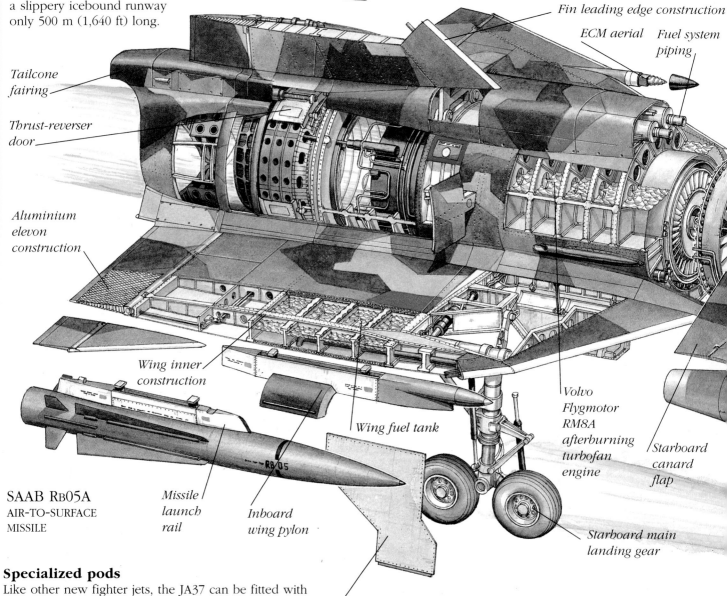

Fin leading edge construction

ECM aerial

Fuel system piping

Tailcone fairing

Thrust-reverser door

Aluminium elevon construction

Wing inner construction

Wing fuel tank

Volvo Flygmotor RM8A afterburning turbofan engine

Starboard canard flap

SAAB RB05A
AIR-TO-SURFACE MISSILE

Missile launch rail

Inboard wing pylon

Starboard main landing gear

Specialized pods
Like other new fighter jets, the JA37 can be fitted with different types of equipment carried in pods under the fuselage. For instance, a reconnaissance version might carry a pod full of cameras. A ground attack version might be fitted with a pod full of electronic warfare equipment to guide bombs and jam enemy signals.

Starboard main landing gear door

Fewer planes, same work
Because of their up-to-date radar and weaponry, a pair of modern jets such as Viggens can do the work of a whole squadron of earlier jet fighters.

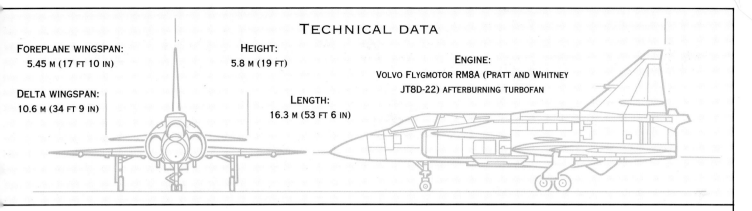

FOREPLANE WINGSPAN:
5.45 M (17 FT 10 IN)

DELTA WINGSPAN:
10.6 M (34 FT 9 IN)

HEIGHT:
5.8 M (19 FT)

LENGTH:
16.3 M (53 FT 6 IN)

ENGINE:
VOLVO FLYGMOTOR RM8A (PRATT AND WHITNEY JT8D-22) AFTERBURNING TURBOFAN

Foreplanes and fin

The Viggen has a large delta wing and foreplanes called canards. They give the plane extra lift and improve manoeuvrability to help it rise up quickly, as it takes off in a short space. The fin can fold down, so that the plane can be stored somewhere with a low roof. Some Viggen hangars are in underground caves.

The cockpit of the future

In the Viggen cockpit three electronic displays give the pilot information without his having to move his head. Designers of modern jets are also trying to cut down on tiring arm movements. In the most up-to-date models all the switches and buttons a pilot uses are located on the control column.

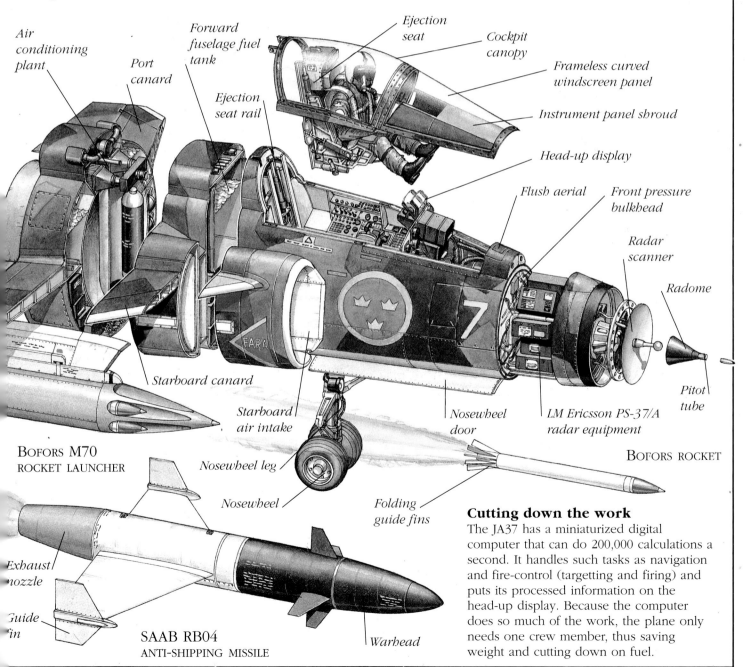

Air conditioning plant

Port canard

Forward fuselage fuel tank

Ejection seat rail

Ejection seat

Cockpit canopy

Frameless curved windscreen panel

Instrument panel shroud

Head-up display

Flush aerial

Front pressure bulkhead

Radar scanner

Radome

Starboard canard

Starboard air intake

Nosewheel door

LM Ericsson PS-37/A radar equipment

Pitot tube

BOFORS M70
ROCKET LAUNCHER

Nosewheel leg

Nosewheel

Folding guide fins

BOFORS ROCKET

Exhaust nozzle

Guide fin

SAAB RB04
ANTI-SHIPPING MISSILE

Warhead

Cutting down the work

The JA37 has a miniaturized digital computer that can do 200,000 calculations a second. It handles such tasks as navigation and fire-control (targetting and firing) and puts its processed information on the head-up display. Because the computer does so much of the work, the plane only needs one crew member, thus saving weight and cutting down on fuel.

MiG-29 FULCRUM

At the British Farnborough air show in 1988 amazed aviation experts got their first glimpse of the Russian MiG-29. They could hardly believe their eyes as they watched it perform aerobatics that should have been impossible for any fighter jet. With abilities like that, an enemy plane chasing a MiG-29 might suddenly find itself zipping helplessly past its quarry as the Russian jet unexpectedly stops in mid-air. It's one of the most agile fighters in the skies, with a range of new ideas that will probably be incorporated into designs of the future.

Pilot helpers

The pilot has two high-tech tools not found in earlier jets. The first is a helmet-mounted gun sight that is attached to the plane's fire-control system. If he wants to, the pilot can direct the plane's targetting laser by simply moving his head. The second is an ejection seat that can save him at low speed and zero altitude.

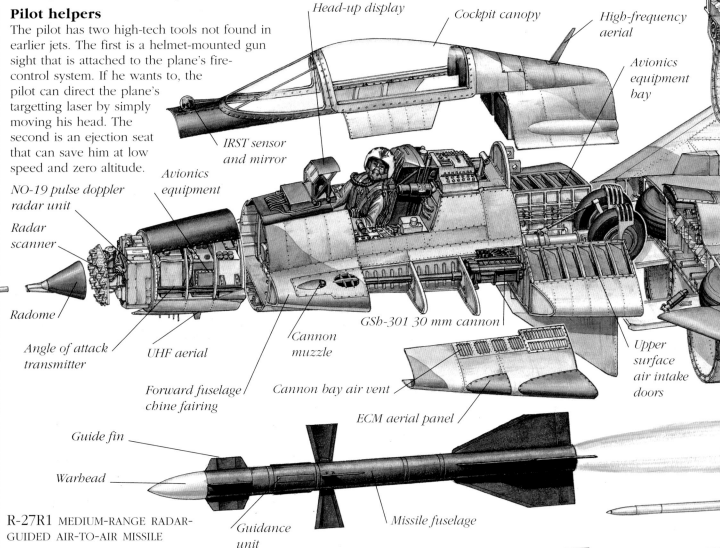

Head-up display

Cockpit canopy

High-frequency aerial

Avionics equipment bay

IRST sensor and mirror

Avionics equipment

NO-19 pulse doppler radar unit

Radar scanner

Radome

Angle of attack transmitter

UHF aerial

Forward fuselage chine fairing

Cannon muzzle

GSh-301 30 mm cannon

Cannon bay air vent

ECM aerial panel

Upper surface air intake doors

Guide fin

Warhead

R-27R1 MEDIUM-RANGE RADAR-GUIDED AIR-TO-AIR MISSILE

Guidance unit

Missile fuselage

Guidance unit

Guide fin

R-73E SHORT-RANGE, INFRA-RED OR RADAR-GUIDED AIR-TO-AIR MISSILE

Magic eye

When a fighter searches the sky with its radar and locks on to a target, it gives its own position away to the enemy. Not so the MiG-29. Ahead of the cockpit there is a glass ball with a mirror inside. The mirror rotates, scanning the sky for thermal signatures (infra-red heat given out by objects). It is called an IRST (Infra-red Search and Track) and it hunts silently, giving out no signals of its own. It is linked to the rest of the fire-control system, so once it finds a target, the plane can attack quickly. The MiG also has conventional radar for ground targets or enemy planes hiding in clouds, when the IRST doesn't work.

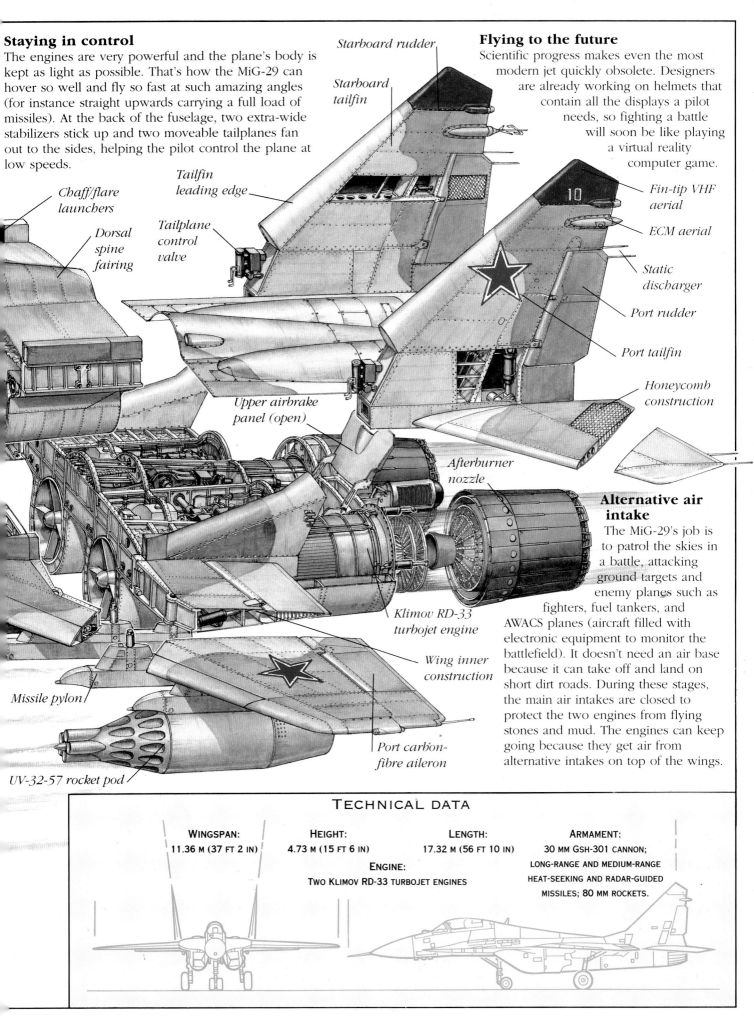

Staying in control

The engines are very powerful and the plane's body is kept as light as possible. That's how the MiG-29 can hover so well and fly so fast at such amazing angles (for instance straight upwards carrying a full load of missiles). At the back of the fuselage, two extra-wide stabilizers stick up and two moveable tailplanes fan out to the sides, helping the pilot control the plane at low speeds.

Chaff/flare launchers

Dorsal spine fairing

Tailfin leading edge

Tailplane control valve

Starboard rudder

Starboard tailfin

Upper airbrake panel (open)

Afterburner nozzle

Klimov RD-33 turbojet engine

Wing inner construction

Missile pylon

Port carbon-fibre aileron

UV-32-57 rocket pod

Flying to the future

Scientific progress makes even the most modern jet quickly obsolete. Designers are already working on helmets that contain all the displays a pilot needs, so fighting a battle will soon be like playing a virtual reality computer game.

Fin-tip VHF aerial

ECM aerial

Static discharger

Port rudder

Port tailfin

Honeycomb construction

Alternative air intake

The MiG-29's job is to patrol the skies in a battle, attacking ground targets and enemy planes such as fighters, fuel tankers, and AWACS planes (aircraft filled with electronic equipment to monitor the battlefield). It doesn't need an air base because it can take off and land on short dirt roads. During these stages, the main air intakes are closed to protect the two engines from flying stones and mud. The engines can keep going because they get air from alternative intakes on top of the wings.

TECHNICAL DATA

WINGSPAN:	HEIGHT:	LENGTH:	ARMAMENT:
11.36 M (37 FT 2 IN)	4.73 M (15 FT 6 IN)	17.32 M (56 FT 10 IN)	30 MM GSH-301 CANNON; LONG-RANGE AND MEDIUM-RANGE HEAT-SEEKING AND RADAR-GUIDED MISSILES; 80 MM ROCKETS.

ENGINE:
TWO KLIMOV RD-33 TURBOJET ENGINES

GLOSSARY

Afterburner
A part at the back of an afterburning jet engine. Inside the afterburner, extra air is burnt with more fuel to boost the engine's power.

Ailerons
Moveable flying control surfaces on aeroplane wings to help keep the plane stable in the air. They control banking and rolling.

Air intake
The opening at the front of a jet engine. Air is drawn in here to feed the jet engines.

Anti-radiation missile
A missile that locks on to an enemy radar source which is emitting signals.

Delta shaped canard

Camouflage
Coloured paintwork on an aeroplane to hide it from enemy view. The colours and patterns vary. For instance, if a plane works over desert it is likely to be painted a sandy colour. In wooded country it is likely to be green and brown.

Chaff
Metal particles that a plane can shoot out behind it. They hang in the air to attract an enemy radar-guided missile away from the plane itself.

Combustion chamber
A space inside an engine where fuel and air are mixed together and burnt.

Compressor
A series of metal vanes that spin around inside the front of a jet engine. They draw in air and squeeze as much as possible into the engine's next stage, the combustion chamber.

Control surfaces
The various wing and tail flaps that make a plane dive or climb, pitch, yaw, or roll.

Delta wing

DELTA WING

Delta wing
A triangular-shaped wing that reduces air resistance at high speeds.

ECM
Initials that stand for **Electronic Counter-measures** – equipment that can jam enemy radar signals.

Elevators
Moveable flaps at the tail of an aeroplane. They can put the plane into a dive or climb.

Elevons
Wing control surfaces on a delta-wing plane that has no tail. They combine the jobs of elevators and ailerons.

Fire-control systems
Equipment for targetting, aiming, and firing weapons.

Flying suit
A pilot's overall, designed to counteract the effects of acceleration forces on the body. If the pilot ejects, it will help protect him from cold and it could contain a waterproof "immersion suit" layer in case the pilot ditches in water.

FLYING SUIT

Fitted helmet or "bone dome"

Oxygen mask

Immersion suit layer

Oxygen supply hose

Life jacket

Map pocket

"Anti-g" trousers

Flying boots

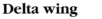

Fly-by-wire
Electronic computerized controls that automatically adjust the various wing and tail flaps on a plane.

Fuselage
The central body of an aeroplane.

"g"
A measurement of acceleration due to gravity, the force that pulls downwards on an aeroplane as it climbs upwards from the Earth's surface.

Ground control
Controllers on the ground who organize and oversee a plane on a mission.

HUD
Initials standing for **head-up display** – the projection of vital information on to the windscreen in front of the pilot.

Heat seeking missile
A missile that locates and locks on to heat emitted by enemy aircraft.

Helmet-up display
Putting all the information that a pilot needs on displays inside his helmet, right in front of his eyes.

FF

Initials that stand for Identification Friend or Foe, a signal on a secret frequency that can only be recognized by friendly forces.

RST

Initials standing for **Infrared Search and Track.** A jet fighter mirror system that scans the sky looking for the heat emissions of enemy aeroplanes.

Laser

Powerful beam of light that can be directed at a target.

Leading edge slats

Control surfaces along the front edge of a wing. These are automatically controlled on modern jets. They help keep the plane stable at low speeds.

Mach number

A way of comparing speed through the air to the speed of sound. Mach 1 is the speed at which sound travels at a given altitude. An aircraft travelling at Mach 1 at sea level would be flying at 1,224.67 km/h (760.98 mph) at a temperature of 15°C (60°F). Above 11,000 m (36,089 ft), Mach 1 is measured as 1,061.81 km/h (659.78 mph).

Nacelle

A streamlined protective pod containing an engine.

Personal location beacon

A military pilot carries this at all times. If the pilot ejects, it activates and sends out signals on an emergency distress frequency, so the pilot can be found and rescued.

Pitot tube

A tube that sticks out of a plane nose or wing and takes in air as the plane flies along. Sensors attached to it measure the air pressure to work out the plane's air speed.

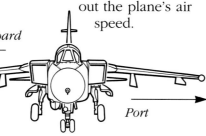

Starboard ←

Port →

Port

Left hand side of the plane (as the pilot looks out of the cockpit). There is a red navigation light on the port wing tip.

Radar

High powered radio pulses that are transmitted, bounce off an object, and return to the receiver.

Rudder

A vertical flying control surface on the tail of a plane.

Starboard

Right hand side of the plane (as the pilot looks out of the cockpit). There is a green navigation light on the starboard wing tip

STOL

Initials that stand for **Short Take Off and Landing,** used to describe a plane that doesn't need a long runway.

TURBOFAN

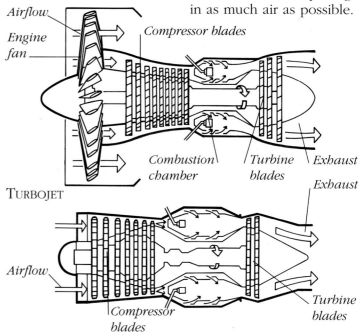

Airflow

Engine fan

Compressor blades

Combustion chamber

Turbine blades

Exhaust

TURBOJET

Airflow

Compressor blades

Exhaust

Turbine blades

Swing wing

(Also called variable geometry wing). A wing that can swing backwards and forwards to change its shape.

Thermal signature

The heat given out by an object.

Turbine

A series of curved metal blades that spin round like a windmill. In a jet engine, exhaust gases spin the turbine, which in turn drives the compressor round.

Turbofan

A turbojet engine with a fan at the front for pulling in as much air as possible.

Turbojet

A jet engine which uses a compressor to feed air into a combustion chamber where it is mixed with fuel and ignited to create thrust.

VTOL

Initials standing for **Vertical Take Off and Landing,** used to describe a plane that can lift straight up into the air or straight down on to the runway.

Thrust directed downwards from jet engine lifts aircraft

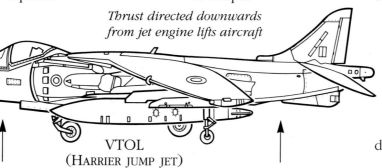

VTOL
(HARRIER JUMP JET)

INDEX

Acknowledgements

Dorling Kindersley would like to thank the following people who helped with the preparation of this book:

Gary Biggin for line artworks
Lynn Bresler for the index
Constance Novis for editorial suppor
Paul Wood for DTP design